Your Limited Company Journey
THE KEY INFORMATION YOU NEED TO KNOW

Your Limited Company Journey

THE KEY INFORMATION YOU NEED TO KNOW

Nigel Reynolds FCCA

Copyright © 2016 Nigel Reynolds

Published by RPN Publishing Limited

The moral right of the author has been asserted according to the Copyright, Designs and Patents Act 1988

All rights reserved. No part of this publication may be reproduced or distributed in any form or by any means, or stored in a database or retrieval system or photocopied, without the prior written permission of the publishers.

Disclaimer: The information provided in this book is for guidance only and it is not intended as either investment advice or to be taken as accounts or tax advice or as legal advice.

Taxation is dynamic and constantly changing, so it is important to always get tax advice based upon the specific business matter you are involved in. Every effort has been taken to compile the contents of this book accurately and carefully. The information provided is correct at the time of writing. However no responsibility for loss occasioned by any person acting or refraining from action as a result of the material in this book can be accepted by the publisher or the author Nigel Reynolds FCCA or the firm Reynolds Accountants Limited T/A Reynolds and Co.

A catalogue card for this book is available from the British Library

ISBN (paperback edition): 978-0-9955099-0-0
ISBN (ebook edition): 978-0-9955099-1-7

Cover design by Slap & Tickle Partnership
Edited by Alison Williams

Publication managed by TJ INK
www.tjink.co.uk

Printed and bound by TJ International in the UK

Contents

Setting Up Your Company	1
Structure of a Limited Company	7
Director Responsibilities and Powers	15
Book-keeping	21
Accounts	27
Audit	33
Extracting Money from the Company	41
Filing Requirements	47
Disclosure	55
Companies House Online Services	59
Groups	65
The Exit	69
Final Words	77
About the Author	80

CHAPTER 1

Setting Up Your Company

Setting Up Your Company

Many people start a business by forming a limited company or having one formed for them. In my experience the problem then is that they usually do not know or do not understand the rules that apply to a limited company.

The purpose of these notes is to demystify that position to allow you to take control of your company and, whilst you may not want to be involved in the detail, at least you will know what to ask for and whether someone is trying to pull the wool over your eyes.

These guidance notes only apply to private limited companies. The rules for public limited companies, companies limited by guarantee and community interest companies, whilst similar in many respects, do have differences not covered in this guide.

Setting up your company

You could go direct to Companies House, and complete the forms there to set up your company. However, in my experience it is quicker and easier to use one of the many on-line company formation agents. The cost of a basic company formation is not that much higher than the fee charged by Companies House.

The company formation agent will electronically submit all of the documentation to Companies House and then provide you with PDF and Word copies of the relevant paperwork. This should include:

- Certificate of Registration – this is the official certificate from Companies House which confirms the company name, whether the company is private or public, date of registration and the registration number of the company.
- Memorandum of Association – this contains the names and signatures of the subscribers (the people forming the company) together with a commitment to take at least one share each.
- Articles of Association– every company must have articles. These are the rules by which the company operates, such as appointing and removing directors as well as issuing shares. A copy of 'Model Articles for a Private Limited Company' can be found at www.gov.uk /guidance/model-articles-of-association-for-limited-companies.
- First Meeting of the Directors Minutes – this confirms the first directors, shareholders, registered office and year end. It also allows the company to make any changes to who is appointed as the directors, secretary or shareholders at the start of the business.
- Company Register – Every company is required to maintain statutory books that record details of the shareholders and the number of shares they hold, together with details of the directors, company secretary and any charges on the company assets.

This is the minimum documentation you should receive.

Rather than setting up the company yourself, you may instead ask your accountant or solicitor to form the company for you. This is particularly important if you want multiple share types or non-standard items in the company articles. Your accountant or solicitor will discuss with you how you want the company structured and then may use a company formation agent to create the company. The solicitor or accountant will ensure that everything is set up correctly and supply you with the finished documentation. This is obviously the most expensive option but will probably be quicker and less stressful than doing it yourself.

CHAPTER 2

Structure of a Limited Company

Structure of a Limited Company

When a Limited Company is formed there are certain things that are needed, for example registered office and directors. It is, therefore, worth having an understanding of what these different things are and their importance.

Name

The name of a limited company must contain the word Limited or Ltd (or its Welsh equivalents 'Cyfyngedig' and 'Cyf') and cannot be the same as any other limited company. In addition the name cannot:

- Be offensive either in total or in part
- Include certain 'sensitive' words or expressions which are included in the regulations
- Use certain characters, signs, symbols and punctuation in the name

The list of sensitive words or expressions as well as the list of characters, signs and symbols are too long to list here but can be found on the Companies House website: https://www.gov.uk/government/publications/incorporation-and-names.

The company can have a trading name which is different to the name listed at Companies House but the same rules apply. The trading name must not include the word 'Limited'.

The registry of business names was disbanded several years ago and there is therefore no longer a Government department with which to register business names. There are several organisations which offer a business names register but membership of them is purely voluntary.

Registered Office

This is the legal address of the company. It does not have to be its trading address and it cannot be a P.O. Box Number. Quite often people will use either their accountant's or solicitor's address rather than their home address, if they would prefer to keep this confidential.

Another option is to use a virtual office address. This is usually provided by one of the serviced office providers. You can find a list of local serviced office providers using an online search.

The registered office is important as it is the address to which all legal documents will be delivered. It is important therefore that if you are using an alternative address (e.g. accountant or virtual office) that you arrange for all correspondence to either be collected daily or forwarded to your home or trading address without delay.

The registered office address must be shown on all official documents and websites. This issue is covered in further detail in chapter nine which covers disclosure of information.

Shareholders

These are the legal owners of the business and there must be at least one shareholder owning at least one ordinary share in the company. There is no upper limit on the number of shares which can be issued, though a private limited company cannot offer shares to the general public; this is something that only public limited companies can do.

A standard company is set up with the ability to issue ordinary shares which have a face value of £1.00 each. However the value of the shares can be whatever you want, starting from £0.01. When the company is first formed it is normal for at least one subscriber share to be issued to either one of the directors or a nominee – this could be the formation agent.

Following on from this, the shareholder(s) can authorise the directors of the company to issue more shares.

There are other types of shares, for example redeemable shares and preference shares, but these are usually only used where there are outside investors. They are not usually issued as part of the normal company structure.

The shareholders are entitled to receive a copy of the company accounts once they have been approved by the directors. They can also be paid dividends by the company, however it is for the directors to decide how much will be paid as dividends. Directors cannot be forced to pay out dividends.

Directors

The directors are responsible for the day to day management of the company and, if a company secretary hasn't been appointed, they are responsible for those duties as well (more details below).

The company must have at least one director. The person appointed as director can also be the only shareholder. Where there is only one director then they cannot also be the company secretary. This isn't a major issue, however, as a private limited company does not have to appoint a secretary.

The directors must ensure that they protect the assets of the company and they cannot compete with the company unless they notify the company and fully disclose all such contracts.

The directors are paid salaries for undertaking their duties. However, they are not subject to the working time regulations and, hence, minimum wage, unless they have a contract of employment.

Company Secretary

Since the introduction of the Companies Act 2006 it has not been necessary for a private limited company to have a company secretary.

Historically all companies had to have a company secretary and where there was only one director of the company, then the company secretary had to be someone else. This usually resulted in the director's husband or wife being appointed as the company secretary in family businesses.

However, when the Companies Act 2006 was being drafted, the then Government woke up to the fact that for most small family businesses, although the wife or husband was named as the company secretary, they actually didn't do anything – the role of company secretary was usually being fulfilled either by the director or the company's external accountant. They made the long overdue and very sensible decision to make the appointment of a company secretary an option for private limited companies.

The traditional role of the company secretary was to:

- File the Annual Return with Companies House
- File the accounts with Companies House
- Submit the Corporation Tax Return and Accounts to HM Revenue & Customs
- Maintain the statutory books
- Call the Annual General Meeting
- Call any other meetings required to be held by the company

These duties are generally undertaken by the external accountant to the company.

Where a company does not appoint a company secretary, then, since the external accountant is not an officer of the company, it is the director's responsibility to make sure those matters are dealt with.

A further change introduced by The Companies Act 2006 was to abolish the Annual General Meeting for private limited companies, directors can hold one voluntarily but they are no longer obliged to do so.

CHAPTER 3

Director Responsibilities and Powers

Director Responsibilities and Powers

The shareholders of the company are the owners of the business but they have no real power as regards the day to day running of the company. The shareholders can appoint and remove the directors of the company however it is the directors who are responsible for the day to day running of the business.

The confusion over this relationship arises because the vast majority of private limited companies have the same people operating both as shareholders and directors. However as mentioned above it is their position as directors where they have the most responsibility.

As directors of a company you are responsible for:

- Acting in accordance with the company's Articles of Association and the directors must promote the company so that it grows and prospers.
- Ensuring that the company maintains adequate accounting records which allow the directors to ascertain within a reasonable period of time what the assets and liabilities of the company are.
- Ensure that the company accounts show a True and Fair View, comply with both Company Law and the appropriate Financial Reporting Standards and if necessary appoint Auditors to audit the annual accounts.

- Not to compete with the company and to disclose to the company if you are involved in any contract which the company is involved in.
- To maintain and protect the company assets. This includes both its tangible assets such as premises, plant and fixtures as well as its less tangible assets such as intellectual property, brand and goodwill.
- Ensure that the company accounts are filed with both Companies House and HM Revenue & Customs no later than the due date for filing.
- Ensure that the Annual Return (soon to be renamed the Confirmation Statement) is filed by its due date.

The powers of the directors include:
- Paying dividends in the company to the shareholders. The shareholders cannot force the directors to pay dividends. This can give rise to conflict between the directors and shareholders where there are shareholders of the company who are not directors.
- Borrow money in the company's name. This power must be exercised in accordance with the Articles of Association.
- Issue additional shares in the company. Again this must be done in accordance with the Articles of Association and with the permission of the existing shareholders.

DIRECTOR RESPONSIBILITIES AND POWERS

The above is an overview of the key responsibilities and duties of directors. Any director should always be mindful of the fact that they can be held personally liable if they breach certain legislation such as Health and Safety regulations.

The directors can also be personally liable if the company trades whilst insolvent. At its simplest level this is where a company is unable to pay its ongoing obligations as they fall due. However this is a very specialist area so anyone concerned regarding whether they are caught by this should contact an Insolvency Practitioner for professional advice and guidance.

CHAPTER 4

Book-keeping

Book-keeping

Keeping accurate records is probably one of the most important parts of any business. In the case of a limited company it is required by legislation in both the Companies Act and also in the Taxes Acts.

The basic requirement of the legislation is that the directors must:

- Show and explain the company's transactions
- Disclose with reasonable accuracy, at any time, the financial position of the company at that time
- Enable the directors to ensure that any accounts required to be prepared comply with both the Companies Act and Accounting Standards.

In addition to the above there is another matter which requires good record keeping and that relates to the payment of dividends. Most company owners will opt for the most tax efficient and legal method of being paid. That is to be paid a low salary and the remainder in dividends. However whilst this ensures that the owners of the business do not pay any more tax than is necessary it leaves them exposed.

If they pay dividends which are later deemed to have been illegal because they failed to show that the company had profits out of which it could pay dividends, the effect of this is that in the event of a liquidation the owners will be asked to repay those dividends to the company. This action could result in them being declared bankrupt if they cannot make the payment.

It is important therefore for the director/owners to be able to show that they reasonably believed that the company was profitable at the time the payments were made. This can only be done with accurate records to support the payment.

The type of records that the company should keep depends upon both the size of the company and the skills of the person keeping the records.

It is much better to keep accurate handwritten records than computer records which are inaccurate and meaningless. Accordingly the directors should consider what they are best able to maintain and also what falls within their own cost structure. Many people today have access to computers and spreadsheets but it is no good using a spreadsheet unless you are confident in your being able to use it accurately.

On that basis the options available to you are:

- A handwritten accounts book, such as Collins Cathedral Accounts Book or Guildhall Accounts Book which allow you to record your income and expenditure on a weekly basis. They also contain summary pages which allow you to monitor performance. Then keep all of your invoices in four files. These would be one for unpaid sales invoices, one for paid sales invoices, one for unpaid purchase and expenditure invoices and one for paid purchase and expenditure invoices. Obviously you will also need a folder for your bank statements. This is the most basic of double entry book-keeping systems but it works.

- A spreadsheet to summarise the income and expenditure on either a weekly or monthly basis, the choice is yours. Together with the folders as mentioned above for the handwritten system. The advantage of this system is that it is low cost and you can easily create a summary page which can then be used to show that the business has made a profit and that dividends can be paid.
- Lastly there are computer accounts packages such as Sage and Xero which are computer and/or cloud based which can help automate transactions and provide you with a list of who owes you money as well as who you owe. Whilst these do have a lot of advantages they also have the disadvantage that if you are not confident in using the system you can rapidly get into a mess. The advantage is that you can generate monthly profit and loss accounts to show that the company has profits available to pay as a dividend. There is one other advantage of the cloud based systems which is that you can give your accountant direct access to the figures so that they can provide you with regular support as well as any support and training you require. Most of these accounts packages also offer training some of which is through free online video's.

The most important factor is that you are using a system that you are comfortable with. You can then monitor the profitability of your business, who owes you money and be compliant for your accounts and HM Revenue & Customs.

It has been stated by some of the high street banks that 80% of small businesses fail within the first three years. This is based upon their own data of accounts being opened and closed. Some of those businesses will have been closed because the owners are not comfortable running their own business and they have got a job instead. A large proportion will have ceased because they ran out of money and a major reason for that is because they did not maintain accurate records and did not realise that they were losing money.

Accurate records are vital to the success of a business without them failure is almost inevitable.

CHAPTER 5

Accounts

Accounts

The accounts of a limited company are required by The Companies Act 2006 to be prepared to show a true and fair view. In addition, they must adhere to either UK GAAP (Financial Reporting Standards) or International Financial Reporting Standards. Most private limited companies have their accounts prepared in accordance with UK GAAP as it is generally more relevant to UK companies.

It is because of the need to comply with a wide range of regulation that companies will usually use the services of a chartered certified accountant or chartered accountant with a practicing certificate.

The amount of information that a company has to disclose to both the shareholders of the company and to the general public through Companies House depends upon the size of the company.

This is currently set as follows:

	Financial Years Starting up to 31/12/2015	Financial Years Starting on or after 1/1/2016
Micro:		
Turnover – up to	632,000	632,000
Balance Sheet Total	316,000	316,000
Average Employees below	10	10
Small – exceeds micro but does not exceed the following:		
Turnover – up to	6,500,000	10,200,000
Balance Sheet Total	3,260,000	5,100,000
Average Employees below	50	50
Medium – exceeds small but does not exceed the following:		
Turnover – up to	25,900,000	36,000,000
Balance Sheet Total	12,900,000	18,000,000
Average Employees below	250	250

In order to qualify for a particular size of company, two out of three of the above criteria must be met. If the company breaches the criteria two years running then they change categories. This is so that companies that have a change in one of the criteria in one year which then reverses the following year are not forced to keep changing their reporting.

The company size criteria will be changing for companies with year ends starting on or after 1 January 2016. This change will reduce the disclosure requirements for many companies but, more importantly, it will mean that a lot of companies will no longer need to have an audit as this is only a requirement for companies that qualify as medium or large.

For small and micro companies it is their choice whether or not to have an audit. However, it should be noted that it only requires shareholders holding 10% of the issued share capital to insist in writing that the company is audited for a small or micro company to be forced to do so. Since having an audit is costly, this is a decision which should not be taken lightly more on audits in chapter six.

CHAPTER 6

Audit

Audit

Most people seem to think that any accountant can undertake an audit and that once they have a limited company then the accounts must be audited. Both of these assumptions are incorrect.

The only people authorised to audit the accounts of a limited company are those Chartered Accountants who hold an auditing certificate. The majority of authorised auditors are members of either the Association of Chartered Certified Accountants (ACCA) or one of the other chartered accountancy bodies such as the Institute of Chartered Accountants in England and Wales (ICAEW). In order to perform an audit the members of these bodies are required to hold both a practicing certificate and also an auditing certificate.

Everyone who is authorised to undertake company audits must appear in the Register of Statutory Auditors. You can verify whether an individual or firm are authorised to undertake audits by searching the register at www.auditregister.org.uk. The audit register site also provides information on how auditors are regulated.

As already mentioned in chapter five the only companies which are required by the Companies Act to have an audit are those which meet the definition of a medium or large company or where they are a member company of a medium or large sized group. Accordingly for small or micro companies there is no legal requirement for them to be audited they may however choose to have an audit or if at least 10% of the shareholders request that an audit be performed.

Before deciding on whether an audit should be undertaken in respect of a small company it is important to have an understanding of what an audit is. In essence an audit is an examination of a company's accounts to ensure that they:

- Give a fair representation of the underlying records
- Comply with the disclosure requirements of the Companies Act
- Comply with the relevant accounting standards
- Show a true and fair view and they are not materially misstated

The auditor will undertake a series of tests on samples of data from the accounting and other records.

Then based upon the results of those tests the auditor will assess whether they can issue a clean report or whether there are issues which will result in a qualified report. The extent of the qualification will be decided by the auditor based upon the type and severity of the issues found. Accordingly it could result in:

- An emphasis of matter – this is simply drawing the readers attention to a particular matter in the accounts of which they should be aware.
- A limitation of scope – this is where the auditor has not been able to satisfy themselves about something in the

accounts because they have been unable to undertake the work they need to do. It could relate to a situation where the directors impose a limit on the work that the auditor can undertake. Alternatively it could be due to the timing of when the auditor is appointed, such as after the year end when the auditor could not then verify the stock at the year end because it is in the past.

Both of the above are what could be considered low level qualifications. The more important ones are:

- Disclaimer of opinion – this would be where the auditor has been unable to obtain evidence for their audit which is so material and pervasive that the auditor has not been able to obtain the evidence they require to express an opinion on the accounts.
- Adverse opinion – this is where the auditor has been able to obtain the evidence they require but the auditor disagrees with the treatment in the accounts such that the auditor believes that the accounts are misleading.

As you can probably appreciate from the above there is a lot of work that the auditor needs to undertake in order to be able to arrive at their opinion and as you may expect that work comes at a cost to the company. The level of cost as you may suspect varies from one auditor to another so it is impossible to give any guidance on the potential cost.

What are the alternatives to an audit? Well that falls under two headings:

- Assurance report – this is a report which is intended to be less detailed than an audit report and to give assurance that the accounts comply with the accounting standards and that the directors are correct in their view that the company does not need an audit. In my opinion the major disadvantages of this report are that it is less understood than the audit report and does not provide any further assurance to outside users of the accounts than the next report which is a compilation report plus it is more costly than the compilation report.
- Compilation report – this is a report confirming that the accountancy firm who sign the report have prepared the accounts from the company records.

Now you have an understanding of what an audit is as well as what the alternatives are the next question is whether there is any disadvantage to not having an audit. The ability of small companies not to be audited has been around for over 20 years. It was phased in starting with companies with a turnover below £95,000 and from 1 January 2016 it will have risen to £10,200,000.

The one effect of this gradual progression is that the credit rating agencies have become accustomed to small companies not being audited and the lack of an audit report no longer seems to have any impact on the company's credit rating. This is probably because the credit companies use alternative information such as payment profiles provided by invoice financing companies as well as information from the courts and the views of company suppliers through web sites setup to rate company payment history.

Since the lack of an audit does not seem to affect the credit rating of the company is it worth having an audit. In my view unless the company is rapidly growing and looking for outside investors the answer is no it isn't worth having an audit. A much better use of the company money would be to pay for a compilation report and then to look for additional services from the accountants to help with such items as:

- Preparation of VAT returns
- Management accounts
- Assessment of the internal controls
- Business coaching or mentoring

All of which will add value to the company and help it grow.

CHAPTER 7

Extracting Money from the Company

Extracting Money from the Company

A question I'm often asked is 'How do I get money out of the company?' This is obviously very important as you have formed the company with a view to making money for yourself, probably to pay your mortgage and provide for your family.

Since a company is a separate legal entity you cannot simply help yourself to the money that is in the company. Well, you could, but that is called a loan and it has tax consequences. The most popular, and simplest, ways to get money out of the company are to be paid a salary or to be paid dividends.

This book is only intended to give you an indication of your options rather than a detailed dissertation on taxation; accordingly you should obtain professional advice on the best solution for you. This will depend upon a combination of your personal circumstances as well as your own attitude to taxation.

With the above in mind:

Salary

If you are in the position of not having any other income, then being paid a salary by the company will allow you to both use your tax free personal allowance to reduce the company profits, thereby saving on corporation tax, and also maintain a credit for national insurance purposes with its associated personal benefits such as a state pension, sick pay and maternity pay.

In order to pay yourself a salary you will need to register with HM Revenue & Customs as an employer. This can either be done through the Government Gateway or at https://www.gov.uk/register-employer. Once you have registered, you will need to process the payroll for the company using either the HM Revenue & Customs payroll service, a bureau service or software such as Sage, Xero or Brightpay. Whichever method you choose, you will have to make RTI (Real Time Information) submissions to HM Revenue & Customs each time you process the payroll.

Dividends

Dividends are paid to the shareholders of the company out of the profits after corporation tax. They do not, therefore, save the company tax. They do, however, save the shareholder paying national insurance. They are therefore an important part of any remuneration structure that you put in place.

In order for the company to pay dividends it must first make profits from which to pay those dividends. If a company pays dividends without having made a profit, then in the event that the company is liquidated the shareholders can be forced to repay those dividends to the company.

It is important then, to show that at the time the company paid the dividends the company had made a profit. This can be done using management accounts.

I'm also frequently asked how often a company can pay dividends. The answer is as often as it likes – it simply has to show that it had profits from which to pay those dividends.

Other methods

There are other methods of extracting money such as director/shareholder loans and using tax avoidance schemes. These all have tax and legal consequences, so professional advice must be taken before these are considered.

CHAPTER 8

Filing Requirements

Filing Requirements

The company is required by the Companies Act 2006 to file certain documents with Companies House and by the Taxes Acts to file a Corporation Tax Return and Accounts with HM Revenue & Customs.

Annual Return (Confirmation Statement)

Every year on the anniversary of the date of its incorporation, the company is required to complete and submit an Annual Return to Companies House and pay the filing fee.

The Annual Return contains the following information:
- Company number
- Company name
- Principal activity – this is denoted by a four digit code number which represents the main activity of the company. Since the company may have more than one activity it is possible to allocate up to four codes. If you cannot find a code that matches your main activity then you can give a written description of the activity and Companies House will select the most appropriate code number.
- Company type – this will be 'private company limited by shares'
- Registered office address

- Location of the statutory records – this is usually selected as the registered office. This is important because any member of the public can request to see the statutory books of any company. Should the company receive such a request, then they must make the statutory books available within a reasonable time period and they may charge a nominal fee
- Company Secretary details – if there is one
- Details of each director
- Statement of Capital – this confirms the type (e.g. 'ordinary), amount paid, amount unpaid, number of shares in issue and the total value of shares in issue for each share type.
- Description of the rights attached to each share type
- Who the shareholders are and the class and number of shares they hold at the annual return date. This is only required every other year unless there has been a change of shareholders during the year.

The Annual Return can be filed either electronically, in which case a fee of £13.00 is payable to Companies House, or in paper form in which case a fee of £30.00 is payable.

The Annual Return must be filed within twenty-eight days of the date to which it is made up, otherwise, as stated in the reminder letter issued by Companies House:

FILING REQUIREMENTS

> Failure to meet the above deadline will result in the Registrar starting the process to strike your company off the register. Please note that it is also a criminal offence not to file an annual return on time. If prosecuted, directors can be fined £5,000.

It is the threat of a fine in the final paragraph which generally ensures that the Annual Return is submitted on time.

The Annual Return will be replaced on 30 June 2016 by a form named Confirmation Statement. The Confirmation Statement will contain the same information currently provided in the Annual Return together with details of the Person with Significant Control (PSC) Register which all companies will have to maintain from 6 April 2016. The other change that is being made is that whilst at present companies are allowed 28 days in which to file the Annual Return they will only be allowed 14 days in which to file the Confirmation Statement.

The PSC Register will have to contain information on individuals who ultimately own or control more than 25% of a company's shares or voting rights or who otherwise exercise control over the company and its management.

This PSC Register will be available to the public who can obtain copies of the Register from the company. The company will be able to charge a fee of £12 for a copy of the register or any part of it.

Accounts

The company must file accounts with Companies House every year. The filing deadline for a private limited company is within nine months of the year end. So a company with a year end of 31 December must file its accounts by the following 30 September.

For small and micro companies the accounts can either be filed electronically in what is called XBRL format, using either proprietary software or, alternatively, using Companies House website software, or they can be filed as paper copies.

Medium sized and large companies must at present file their accounts as paper copies – there is no facility for them to file their accounts electronically.

Eventually, once Companies House have sorted out their issues with accepting all sized company accounts, they will stop accepting paper copies for filing, but at present they offer both facilities for small and micro companies.

If the accounts are not filed at Companies House by the filing deadline then there are penalties for being late. The penalties at this time are:

Not more than one month late	£150
More than one month but not more than three months	£375
More than three months but not more than six months	£750
More than six months	£1,500

These penalties are doubled where the company is late in filing their accounts in two successive years.

Corporation Tax Return

The company is required to pay its corporation tax within nine months and one day of its year end but it is not required to file its Corporation Tax Return and accounts with HM Revenue & Customs until twelve months after its year end. It can file the Corporation Tax Return and Accounts early but filing late will lead to penalties as follows:

One day late – £100
Three months late, a further – £100
Six months late – HMRC will estimate the tax due and charge a 10% penalty
Twelve months late, a further 10% penalty

In the case of these penalties, if you are late three times then the penalty for both the one day and three months changes from a £100 penalty to a £500 penalty. Definitely not to be recommended.

CHAPTER 9

Disclosure

Disclosure

Under Company Law all companies must disclose certain information about themselves. The disclosure provisions apply equally to both printed matter and electronic documents (e.g. email and websites) and advertising.

The information to be disclosed can be summarised as follows:

1. **Outside every office or place in which its business is carried on**
   - Name
2. **Letterheads and order forms (hard copy or electronic)**
   - Name
   - Registered office
   - Registered in England and Wales or Registered in Scotland
   - Registered number
3. **Invoices and receipts (hard copy or electronic)**
   - Name
   - VAT number
4. **Websites and e-mails**
   - Same as for letterheads and order forms
5. **All other notices and publications**
   - Name

One important point to note is that it is not necessary to show the names of the directors or the company secretary in any of the above. However, if the company should disclose the names of the directors or company secretary then it must show the names of **all** the directors and the company secretary – it cannot be selective.

It is totally incorrect that you have to disclose your VAT registration number if you are registered on your website or all documentation. The only place where a VAT registration number is required to appear is on a VAT invoice.

CHAPTER 10

Companies House Online Services

Companies House Online Services

Using the Companies House online services can be invaluable as you can use it to verify that documents have been filed and, if you want to manage the filing of documents yourself rather than using your accountant or other agent, then you can complete and submit the relevant document yourself.

The most popular items to file with Companies House are:
- AR01 – Annual Return
- AP01 – appoint a director
- AP03 – appoint a secretary
- CH01 – change the details of a director
- CH03 – change the details of a secretary
- TM01 – terminate an appointment of a director
- TM02 – terminate an appointment of a secretary
- AD01 – change a registered office address

The major advantages of filing the above documents electronically are:
- the documents cannot get lost in the post
- they appear on the company register more quickly
- you get an email confirming that the document has been submitted

Using this service does, therefore, give greater assurance to the directors of the company.

PROOF

You're probably thinking proof of what? Well PROOF actually stands for Protected Online Filing and is a system setup by Companies House to make it more difficult to steal a corporate identity.

The system requires that documents must be filed electronically and have some personal security information attached to them.

The personal information must be any three items from the following list:

Town of birth	– First three letters
Telephone number	– Last three digits
National Insurance number	– Last three characters
Passport number	– Last three digits
Mother's maiden name	– First three letters
Eye colour	– First three letters
Father's first name	– First three letters

With the increase in identity theft both personal and corporate, this is invaluable protection for the company and its directors.

The company can sign up to PROOF simply by the directors registering to use the online filing service of Companies House. Once registered with the online service, simply log into that service and then:

1. Select the 'Join PROOF' link near the padlock icon at the top of the overview screen
2. Agree to the Terms and Conditions
3. Select 'Protect this company'.

Having completed the above you will receive an email confirming that your application has been successful.

CHAPTER 11

Groups

Groups

For many people the term 'group of companies' suggests a large public limited company. However in reality there are a large number of small groups of companies.

A group is basically where one company owns another. This can be done for a variety of reasons but the most popular ones are:

- Where one company buys another company.
- For reasons of geography. For example where a business is located in England and also Scotland. The owners may choose to have the different operations as separate companies but have them under common ownership as a group.
- For marketing reasons. The company may operate in two different markets e.g. consultancy and manufacturing. It may therefore be better for the marketing of both operations to be set up as separate companies.

Setting businesses up in a group may also be done for other commercial reasons such as to more easily monitor the profitability of a particular business and also to set profit-sharing arrangements with senior management. It could also make it easier to sell one of the companies within the group. The company will already have separate records and therefore trading results won't need to be separated.

There are also tax advantages to operating as a group rather than having each company owned directly by the shareholders. Where the group company is seventy-five per cent or more owned by another company in the group then losses incurred by one company can be relieved against the profits of another.

Lastly, there are no issues in a group structure of one company supporting another by lending it money. Where there are two companies owned separately by the same shareholders, then this can give rise to deemed 'loans to participators' which will then give rise to both benefit in kind charges as well as tax charges under s455 Corporation Taxes Act 2010.

The downside of one group company lending to another, is that if that company fails and goes into liquidation then it can bring down the whole group. In such circumstances careful planning and control is required.

CHAPTER 12

The Exit

The Exit

I had thought of calling this section 'the death of the company' but that sounded way too dramatic. Yet when a company is struck-off or liquidated it does, in effect, die. But that isn't the only way that you may cease to be involved with the company. Other options include:

- Passing to the next generation
- Selling the company
- Striking off by Companies House
- Striking off at Companies House by you
- Administration and liquidation

All of the above result in you no longer having an involvement with the company.

Selling or passing to the next generation

I have put these two together because they have many similarities. Whether passing a company to the next generation or selling the company, the first thing to remember is that it is not something that you can simply wake up one morning and do. It takes time to select and groom the person or people who will take over just as much as it takes time to groom a company before you sell it.

This process will take longer than you probably think.

With a successor I would recommend at least three to five years. The reason for this time frame is so that they can be trained in all of the areas where they lack experience, such as company finance as well as staff management, then there is also making sure they meet with and get to know all of the key customers as well as the key suppliers.

Most people only look at one aspect of what they themselves do and assume that their successor will pick up the rest as they go. They may be able to pick up the additional knowledge but it will take time and hold back the company. Don't take the risk; do the job properly and make sure that they have all the skills they need to replace you.

You also need to consider how you are going to receive money from the company. Is the company cash rich – meaning you can simply sell your shares back to the company? Will the company need to raise money by borrowing against its assets or will it buy you out over time, either through a consultancy agreement or as an earn-out? All of this needs careful planning not only to ensure that the company continues after you are no longer involved, but also to ensure you get paid as much as possible for your shares and pay as little tax as possible.

Selling the company to a third party who has no knowledge of the company requires even more planning and I would recommend starting at least five to ten years ahead of the sale. Now your initial reaction might be that this is unreasonable. However, you need to remember that your strategy to date has probably been to minimise the tax you have to pay and to extract as much money from the business as you can. Such a strategy does not necessarily produce a company or accounts that look very appealing to a buyer. It is therefore important to start planning well in advance of the sale to clear out any skeletons in the company and make it look 'sexier' for a buyer.

I will not go further into the mechanics or strategy of selling a company because this book is only to give you a flavour of various matters relating to owning and operating a company. Having said that, I can clearly remember working on the sale of two businesses where the owners decided to sell at short notice.

In the case of the first, the offer price was £7 million but during due diligence some issues were found with the pricing of goods as well as stock values. The owner tried to cover this with items that had never been included in the accounts as assets. The buyer didn't accept this argument and the business ended up being sold for £3 million.

In the second case the owner again woke up one morning and decided to sell. The original offer price was £20 million but the purchaser found some negative items in the accounts. The owner claimed that certain expenses would no longer be paid by the company so the company was actually worth £60 million. This strategy failed miserably and the company was sold for £13 million.

In both of these cases, with advanced planning, the original price could have been achieved – if not more.

Striking a Company Off

As explained above, this can either be done by Companies House applying for the company to be struck off or through the owners applying for it to be struck off.

Companies House will take action to strike a company off when the company has failed to meet its filing requirements either as regards its Annual Return or accounts. A formal notice that the company is being struck off will be sent by Companies House to both the company and the directors. The whole process takes about two months.

The directors of a company can apply for it to be struck off by Companies House. This costs £10.00 and is usually done because the company is no longer trading and is not required. Again, this usually takes about two months.

The key point to remember here is that where a company is struck off and has assets, then those assets become the property of the Crowns Solicitor; they do not pass to the shareholders or directors.

If a company is struck off with assets or struck off by Companies House because documents have not been filed then it is possible to get the company re-instated to the Register. There are firms of solicitors who specialise in this, although it can be costly as there are the fees to be paid to the solicitors as well as paying any outstanding penalties to Companies House. The process usually takes between six and nine months to achieve so it is best avoided.

Administration/Liquidation

Most people think of this happening only when a company is in difficulty, but it can occur when a company's owners no longer want to trade the company and do not want to sell it. The company is formally wound up in order to release cash and assets.

It doesn't matter whether this process is at the decision of the owners or because of something bad befalling the company (e.g. a large customer not paying them) – it will always be handled by an insolvency practitioner authorised to deal with this process.

CHAPTER 13

Final Words

Final Words

In writing this book I set out to provide the basic information needed in order to comply with the legal regulations to set up, manage and if needs be close a company. Hopefully you will now have a better understanding of what is required of you.

As I have heard so many times in the past 'knowledge is power' but it also moves you from the dark into the light. So you should now feel more secure knowing what is expected of you and you can now focus on building a prosperous business for you and your family.

About the author

A professional accountant with over thirty years' experience, much of it gained through working with owner-managed businesses, Nigel Reynolds has a wealth of knowledge and expertise.

He has worked in both professional practices and in industry and has seen many sides of business. His experience of working with those just starting out, as well as seasoned business owners, and his interest in property taxation and family run enterprises, means he has a detailed understanding of the challenges faced by small businesses.

Nigel specialises in business investment and development and regularly gives talks on the different tax aspects of investing in or developing property.

He is a director of Reynolds and Co which he jointly founded with the sole objective of working with owner-managed businesses.

Nigel can be contacted at nigelreynolds@reynoldsandco.co.uk

Notes